Hamish McFee

GH00381938

By

Barry Crossby

This book is dedicated to the late Brenda Strivens a wonderful lady and dedicated West Highland Terrier Breeder

Contents

PROLOGUE

Sitting down in our lounge on a cold bleak winter's day at the end of 2020 with a blank sheet of paper and pen at the ready we asked ourselves the question *"What are we trying to achieve in writing this story about our personal dog experience?"* Of course all dog owners reading this book will be shouting the answer *"It's getting the message across in words how you share a part of your life with an animal that does not speak but provides loyalty, companionship and love".*

Looking back on my childhood and reflecting I can recall that apart from owning a hamster and goldfish I was not brought up in a doggy household. In fact at an early age I was chased by an Alsatian which left a lasting impression and made me frightened to be near any dog. With hindsight I am sure that the dog just wanted to play with me. Margaret was also not brought up with dogs and only has fond memories of having a guinea pig.

As we now realise not having the companionship of a dog throughout our childhood's was a great loss and it has taken over 40 years to correct.

Every year when we get our new calendar we always make a note of birthdays and special events for the year ahead. One date in particular the 10th April 2017 will always stand out as it was the day we lost our beloved West Highland Terrier Hamish McFee.

Four years has now past and our tears has now given way to all the wonderful memories of Hamish and what he brought to our lives and countless other people during his 16 year life.

Hamish was primarily a family pet but what he achieved during his life as a Pets As Therapy dog is truly outstanding and something that deserves to be shared.

Every day Hamish is still in our thoughts and we hope all readers of this story will enjoy it as much as we enjoyed writing it.

As you will discover reading this story the bond between a dog and humans cannot easily put into words but it is without doubt a rewarding experience and one that will remain with us for the rest of my lives.

So with this in mind this is our story about a West Highland Terrier that came into our lives in the spring of 2001.

Chapter One –
Finding Hamish

Entering a new millennium in 2000 life was good for Margaret and me. We both had good jobs mine as a Civil Engineer in Local Government and Margaret working in mental health care and we had been happily married for 22 years. Hobbies occupied a lot of our time I was playing the drums in a band and Margaret attending to her allotment. My stepson was forging his own way in life and it was now the time to start enjoying the fruits of our labours.

I thought we had everything we needed but this was to dramatically change when out of the blue one evening over dinner Margaret said *"we should get a dog"*. Nothing more was said that evening but on reflection I recall having mixed emotions was something lacking in our relationship, why did we need a dog. I lay in bed for several nights thinking how I approach this knowing Margaret was determined and it wasn't going to go away.

A few weeks later we were out enjoying a stroll in the winter sunshine when Margaret pointed to a dog walker and said *"that's the dog I would like"*. It was a black Scottish Terrier but Margaret called it a Westie. Not knowing anything about dog breeds I did a Google search and quickly realised Margaret meant she wanted a West Highland Terrier and not a Scottie.

At this point I knew I was backing myself into a corner and thought the only way to resolve this was to search westie breeders and ask for some advice which if I am honest would result in us not being deemed suitable for dog ownership.

In late November on a bleak winter's day I downloaded a list of West Highland Terrier breeders throughout the UK and recognised a dialling code which was one digit away from my mother-in-laws phone number in Hastings. I dialled the number with some trepidation and after what seemed a lifetime a lady answered the phone *"Mrs Corry speaking, how may I help"* I replied *" My name is Mr Crossby and I am sorry to trouble you but we are thinking of getting a Westie and could you please offer us some advice"*. Without any hesitation Mrs Corry replied *"Two things Mr Crossby one you have phoned North Yorkshire and two I don't have any Westie puppies available at the present time"*. By this time I felt rather stupid but later realised that one different digit in a dialling code can result in a call to a completely different part of the UK. However Mrs Corry was very helpful and suggested that I phone her friend in Sussex a Brenda Strivens who would be able to offer us some advice.

After thanking Mrs Corry I dialled the phone number provided and outlined to Brenda who I was and asking if she had any westies for sale. The response back was not what I expected and for what seemed like a lifetime she gave me a lecture on how she did not breed puppies for Christmas and had no intention of doing so. After this dressing down I thought the phone call would be abruptly ended but I remembered the saying that was often in the news that "a dog is for life not just Christmas". I quickly replied that we were only looking for advice and did not want a puppy for Christmas. I also made it clear that we had not owned a dog before and this was just an enquiry

Brenda's attitude then changed dramatically and she informed me that that one of her westies named Jeanie was expecting puppies in January and she would contact us again after the birth and arrange for us to visit her and see the puppies.

Margaret was over the moon with this news and I thought it would be a good idea to get some books out of the library on West Highland Terriers as I wanted to be prepared for our visit to meet Brenda.

The books I read were useful and even I was now warming to the idea of owning dog. One interesting bit of advice stated that if you are choosing a puppy from a litter you should ask to see them on your own in a separate room and choose the one that comes to you. This is meant to be a good indication but I knew that Margaret only wanted a boy so our choice could be limited.

Christmas 2000 was like any other Christmas for us and entailed entertaining our elderly parents and in some respects it was good to step back from the idea of having a puppy as I was under no illusion a puppy would be life changing for us and the final decision should be rational and not just based on seeing a cute puppy that clearly would melt anybodies heart.

Early in the New Year our minds went back to being told we would get a phone call and I was beginning to think that maybe it wouldn't happen but sure enough on the 6th January 2001 we got that phone call which was very short and to the point

"Mrs Strivens speaking just to let you know Jeanie has had a litter of eight puppies and I will arrange for you to visit me for a chat when they are four weeks old".

It may have been a short and to the point phone call but it lifted our spirits and we couldn't wait to get the next phone call so we could see the puppies and find out if we would be suitable owners.

Hamish with those mesmerising eyes

Chapter Two –
Meeting the Breeder

I must admit that the thought of seeing the westie puppies was starting to excite me as well and we were both longing for the day when the breeder would contact us. As promised we did get a phone call and a date was agreed for us to make a visit,

Neither of us knew what to expect when we arrived at the breeders house so we just rung the bell and waited for a response. The silence of our arrival was quickly replaced with the sounds of dogs barking and as the door opened two westies came bounding at us. My immediate reaction was to put my hand on the dogs head to pat it and that was my first mistake *"Don't do that shouted Mrs Strivens, putting your hand on a dogs head is a sign of aggression"*. Before I could react I was told when first meeting a dog you should stroke the dog under the chin and let it smell your hand. Oh Dear I thought that was not a good start and my first black mark. However, we were invited in and proceeded to go into the kitchen when I noticed along the walls of the hallway were numerous rosettes and certificates. I asked Brenda what were they awarded for and she explained they were awards her westies had received at dog shows including Crufts. We must have spent at least half an hour looking at all of them and it was clear that we were in the company of a very competent breeder.

In the kitchen over coffee it was explained that the puppies were in a special enclosure which could be divided into two so the mum could have the occasional rest away from the lively westie pups.

At last we were allowed to see the puppies and there before our eyes were eight puppies with mum Jeanie watching their every move. Brenda opened the cage housing the puppies and that's when I made my second mistake of the day. I went to stroke the first puppy Brenda was holding and I was immediately told not to do that as another human scent could result in the mum rejecting the puppy. Clearly another black mark and I was starting to think that we had blown it. The puppies were of course absolutely gorgeous and would have melted anybodies heart.

Back in the kitchen we continued to chat and I was trying to build up the courage to ask two questions *did she think we would be suitable to have one of the puppies and how much would the puppy be.* Finally I managed to ask my two questions. Without hesitation Brenda confirmed that each puppy was £600 and yes she thought we would be suitable owners but would have to visit our house and garden to check it was suitable.

Now the last question I had was did we have a choice of what puppy we could have remembering the advice I had read about seeing which puppy came to you. The answer I got was again not one I was expecting as Brenda said that she always matched the right puppy to all prospective owners and in our case as never having had a dog before we needed a calm westie. A date was fixed for our home visit and was informed that Jeanie and one or two of the puppies would come to our house as well.

Before we left for home we had one final look at all the puppies and I remember that there was one puppy sleeping at the back of the cage which Brenda could not reach. It crossed my mind many years later that the puppy could have been Hamish.

Our heads were now spinning with all the information was had gained but it was worthwhile and more to the point we had been provisionally accepted as being suitable to own one of Mrs Strivens westies. We chatted all the way home and both realised that our lives would now change but the future seemed exciting and we hoped our home visit would go well.

Puppy Hamish

Chapter Three – Home Visit & Collecting Hamish

It seemed an endless amount of time waiting for our home visit rather like the anticipation of a child waiting for Christmas Day to arrive. We both wanted to make a good impression on Mrs Strivens and spent endless hours cleaning the house and making sure all the fencing in our garden was secure and escape proof for an inquisitive puppy.

We certainly could do no more and we waited patiently for the agreed day of our home visit. I must admit when the day arrived I was constantly looking out of the window when a gleaming silver Volvo Estate pulled up outside our house. I went straight out to meet Mrs Strivens and immediately saw that there were two cages in the back of her car. Mrs Strivens explained that she wanted Jeanie to leave her scent in our garden and to my excitement the other cage contained two puppies one I assumes was going to be our westie. Once we were safely inside the house the cages were opened and the two puppies came bounding out and went straight into the garden closely watched by their mum.

Fortunately Mr Strivens was happy with our house and deemed our garden a safe place for a boisterous puppy to play. We got the news that the male puppy she brought was going to be our puppy and seeing the two puppies together ours did seem the quieter of the two.

We had debated for several days what name to call our puppy and Margaret remembered a bedtime story that her father had told her when she was a child about getting a bus to the moon where Mr McFee would be waiting for you. Margaret also told me that her favourite Scottish name was Hamish. So there it was our Westie was going to be named Hamish McFee.

Having met Mrs Strivens requirements to have one of her puppies we agreed a date to collect Hamish when he would be nine weeks old and ready to become a part of our lives. We were so excited and couldn't wait for the day to arrive that would then go on to change our lives for the next 16 years in more ways than we could have ever imagined.

The day finally arrived to go and collect Hamish and bring him home. We woke to a bright sunny day and spent some time discussing how our lives were going to change having a nine week old puppy to look after. We agreed with Brenda that we would arrive after lunch and to make sure we weren't late we decided to leave early and stop for lunch at a pub on the way. Over lunch I noticed a number of well behaved dogs lying under tables and thought to myself that could be Hamish in a few months time relaxing in a pub with us after a long walk.

When we knocked at Brenda's door this time I was hoping to get a brownie point by greeting her westies the right way but this time there were no westies and we went straight through to the kitchen for coffee. Over coffee Brenda explained that she would give us an information sheet on looking after Hamish and that he would initially need four small meals a day while he was growing up.

In addition Brenda gave us a piece of cloth with the scent of Hamish's mum on it which we could put in his bed.

We had already decided to keep Hamish in our kitchen at night whilst he was being house trained and Brenda was happy with this decision as our kitchen had a glass door so that Hamish would be able to see out and not feel trapped.

Brenda also gave us another tip that we should continue to lay newspaper on the floor and gradually move it to the back door. At that point we should take Hamish out into the garden and once he had been to the toilet we should praise him and bring him back in the house. The idea behind this is that Hamish would then realise that the garden is for using as a toilet and not just for playing.

We were both reaching a point of information overload when Brenda said she would go and get Hamish. When we set eyes on Hamish he seemed so small in Brenda's arms and I remember those big black eyes looking straight at me which would have melted anybodies heart. It was a moment to savour thinking how Brenda had given me a lecture when I first contacted her and now three months later we were going to hold our own westie.

It was now time to get Hamish back home and kindly Brenda said if we had any concerns over Hamish in the future we could phone her. She said she would also stay in touch to see how Hamish was progressing. We felt reassured by this as we knew we were novice owners and wanted to do everything we could to look after Hamish properly.

To keep Hamish safe getting him home in the car we had bought a cage but when Brenda saw this she was not impressed and told Margaret to sit in the back of the car and hold Hamish as this would be his first bonding with us as his new owners

Brenda kindly gave us a gift before we left, a small cushion with the wording "A dog and his house keeping assistance live here".

How true that was going to turn out for us and would take us on a journey for the next 16 years from the main arena at Crufts to the Daily Mirror Animal Hero Awards at the Langham Hotel in London and many more adventures and events in between.

A gleaming white Hamish so cute

Chapter Four –
Early Days

One thing you realise very quickly is that a puppy has boundless energy and the next minute they crash out in a deep sleep. Brenda did warn us that the first night Hamish would probably cry for his mum but he would soon adapt to having human parents. It had been a long day collecting Hamish and after exploring all the nooks and crannies in our house and garden we decided to have an early night and left Hamish in our kitchen with his bed and toys. We must have fallen into a deep sleep but I was woken up by a whimpering sound from downstairs which was of course Hamish. I listened for what seemed a lifetime and remembered what Brenda had told us. The only problem was it tugged at my heart strings so much but I had to go and see if he was ok. Hamish was wide awake and he was so excited to see me I could not leave him on his own so out came my sleeping bag and we both snuggled up together. Hamish was happy but my back the next day was certainly not and I also accepted I had made my first mistake but what could I do knowing Hamish was still missing his mum and the rest of the litter. The strange thing was it never happened again and I think it was my first real bonding session with Hamish.

As the weeks past we began to get into a routine and we started to realise the significance of the wording on the cushion Brenda had given us "a dog and his house keeping assistance live here". We both joked who was going to end up the boss and of course it would be Hamish Mc Fee.

Brenda had told us that we would need to register Hamish with our local vet and arrange for him to have his remaining injections. Like any new puppy all the vet's nurses fell in love with Hamish and all wanted to hold him. The vet examined Hamish all over and informed us that one of his testicles had not descended and would need to have a minor operation to remove it from the abdomen as it could become cancerous in later life. This was not the news we wanted to hear but the vet re-assured us that it was a routine operation and there was unlikely to be any complications. When we got home we phoned Brenda who explained that it was a very common occurrence with West Highland Terriers and it was a very safe operation.

The day of the operation arrived and we were so worried that Hamish would be ok. The nurse took Hamish away and we were told to phone back after six hours to check how he was. We were both so worried by then that we just couldn't concentrate on anything else and just wanted time to race by.

Time just seemed to slow up and eventually we phoned the vet who fortunately informed us that Hamish was fine and we could go and collect him. We were so pleased to see him and realised what he already meant to us. The vet told us to just let him rest and give him a light meal of a scrambled egg and by the morning he would be fine. The effect of putting Hamish to sleep had not really worn off and Hamish was a bit unsteady on his feet but fortunately he just wanted to sleep and recover from his operation.

The next day we woke up and Hamish was wandering around the bedroom and we thought was something wrong and then we realised that he hadn't eaten for a day.

He was certainly hungry and devoured two meals at once and Margaret joked typical a man only thinks of his stomach! Well in this case we were just pleased to see Hamish was ok and within a few days it was like nothing

13

had happened and he was back being our Hamish again. I think maybe having an operation at such a young age gave Hamish a fear of visiting the vet because as he got older he was not at all happy in the company of a vet and shall we say he just tolerated it. Mind you he never refused a treat from the vet!

Hamish of course still had to have his remaining injections but the time quickly arrived when Hamish had had all his injection at the vet and we were able to take him to our local park for his first proper walk with us.

From my reading of the book I had on Westies I knew it would take time to get the confidence to let Hamish off the lead and I was really concerned that Hamish would run off. It must have shown that I was nervous as I meet a lady who was walking with her spaniel off the lead and she stopped me and said *"you are new to this aren't you"* I replied *"yes"* The response I got was not what I was expecting as she firmly said to me *"take that dog of the lead he will be ok and just play with my dog"* I felt like a naughty school boy and just did what I was told. Hamish of course loved every minute being free from the lead and had a wonderful time with the ladies spaniel.

I had meet my first dog walking friend and you quickly realise that with a dog people stop and chat and we continued to make more friends with dog walkers and regularly meet up so all the dogs could socialise and play together.

One dog owner I met in our park was a local postman Russell who had a small Jack Russell dog named Freddie. Hamish and Freddie seemed to have an instant bond and Freddie seemed to be very protective towards Hamish. This proved itself to be very true when one Sunday morning Hamish was running around with Freddie when a rather large Alsatian came bounding towards Hamish.

Before I could react Freddie intervened and loudly barked at the Alsatian who immediately stopped and then ran away. From that point on Freddie was then known to all as "Hamish's bodyguard".

Russell also referred to Hamish as "Houdini Hamish" following one of our Sunday walks. As usual Freddie and Hamish were walking alongside us when we realised Hamish was nowhere to be seen. He was behind us and then just vanished.

We immediately started searching the adjoining hedges and calling out Hamish's name when all of a sudden he popped out of the hedge some 20 metres from where we were standing. To this day we never know how Hamish managed to slip by us without us noticing and hence the name "Houdini Hamish"

This was such a happy time for both of us and we started to realise that nothing seemed to faze Hamish and Brenda had without doubt chosen the right puppy for us.

I thought back to seeing the puppies for the first time in Brenda's house and remembered the westie at the back of the cage on his own. Surly that was Hamish the quiet laid back westie!

Every week Hamish was now putting on weight and developing into a very cute westie. Our confidence as virgin dog owners was also growing and we felt the time was right to take Hamish away on his first holiday at the tender age of eight months. Self catering seemed to be the obvious choice and the Isle of Wight was top of our list as it was somewhere we had numerous happy holidays in the past with our son.

Beach Boy Hamish

♪♪ Beach baby,beach baby there on the sand,from July to the end of September.♫

Chapter Five –
Holiday and TV appeal

We wanted a fairly rural location with plenty of open space for Hamish to run around and found the perfect holiday cottage near the village of Godshill. I remember getting our cases out for packing and before I knew it Hamish jumped into one of the cases. I think he was making a statement *"if you are going somewhere so am I"*. However, he did seem happier when his bed and toys were loaded in the car and on what was a beautiful summers day in June we set off to catch the IOW ferry from Portsmouth. Life could not have been any better with the thought of spending time with Hamish on our first holiday together.

Already knowing the layout of the cottage we had rented we had decided to put Hamish's bed in the kitchen at night and we would be in the adjoining bedroom. We thought this would be a good plan but it didn't cross our minds that being in a rural area there was no street lighting at night and the first night it was completely dark. Hamish didn't seem to be fazed by this at first and we all settled down for night. However, it wasn't long before there was scratching on our bedroom door and when I opened it Hamish launched himself onto our bed where he stayed the rest of the night quite happy. The next day we realised that Hamish was not use to a dark room at night and we decided it would be best to put Hamish's bed in our room but if I am honest he spent most of the week on our bed.

There was a nice village pub in Godshill that allowed dogs in the bar area so we decided to give Hamish his first experience of being in a busy pub. To tell you the true he was very calm in the pub and just lay under our table not even worrying us when the food was served. In reality his calmness was probably due to all the long walks we were having and Hamish was probably glad just to chill out and enjoy the rest. It also took me back to the day we collected Hamish and stopping off for an early pub lunch where they were a lot of well behaved dogs and now we had a well behaved Westie as well.

I am sure that all dog owners will agree that when you have a dog people often stop and have a chat when you are out or just smile when you walk by. In the afternoons we would stop off at a beach cafe for a cup of tea and to give Hamish a well earned rest. On the penultimate day of our holiday we were at a cafe in Ryde enjoying the afternoon sun and we noticed two tables away was a gentleman with two adult westies. It wasn't long before we started talking to each other and found out that the gentleman's name was Jim. He wanted to know all about Hamish and it turned out that he was a fountain of knowledge and told us he had had westies most of his life. Before we headed back to our accommodation we exchanged telephone numbers and said we would stay in touch. Over the years Jim has become a good friend and we have both valued his help and advice on caring and looking after westies.

We spent the odd day touring the Isle of Wight and finding new open spaces where Hamish could enjoy himself off the lead he seemed so happy rolling in the long grass, a happy and carefree puppy enjoying life.

On our travels we stopped at a corner shop to stock up on a few groceries and Margaret went into the shop while I waited outside with Hamish. I hadn't been standing their long when a lady came up to me and asked some questions about how old Hamish was and where we had come from. The lady then asked if I wanted to go into the shop she would hold him for me. I politely declined her offer but updating Margaret we then realised that the lady could have been genuine but on the other hand she may have stolen Hamish. A frightening thought and I then remembered that our Breeder had warned me never to leave Hamish unattended in a car or leave him with a stranger. Thank goodness I had heeded that warning.

There was no chance of a lie in with Hamish who just wanting to be out and about so we used to just catch up with breakfast television. As it happened this turned out to be a defining moment in what Hamish was going to achieve over the course of the next fifteen years. One of the TV items was an appeal for a charity named Pets As Therapy. The appeal told the story of a young child that had to go into hospital every day for an injection. Being so afraid of needles it took over an hour every time to administer the injection. One of the nurses had the idea of bringing along a Pets As Therapy dog which may distract the child and make them more relaxed. Sure enough the child was besotted with the dog and didn't even know that the injection had taken place.

I remember at this point turning to Margaret and saying *"that was wonderful to see and what a worthwhile charity"*. I went on to say *"Hamish could do that, he is a calm dog and you work in a hospital in Croydon, let's look into it when we get home"*.

Chapter Six –
The Saga of Grooming and Puppy Training

Hamish was now approaching nine months and his fur was rapidly growing so we thought it was time to have Hamish trimmed, but where? I asked our local dog walking friends who recommended a lady that lived close to us. We contacted the lady and duly made an appointment and dropped him off at her house. Nearly three hours past by when the phone rang and to our surprise she said that Hamish had not stopped barking and she had done the best she could. In fact Hamish now looked more like a poodle than a westie so we needed to find somebody else. In my westie book the classic westie haircut is to have the head shaped like a chrysanthemum flower, the tail in the shape of a carrot and a skirt left at the sides. It certainly was a great look but clearly required a large amount of skill to achieve it. Further enquiries resulted in obtaining the contact details of Lynn another local dog trimmer who turned out to be the complete opposite of the first groomer we had used. Lynn was brilliant with making dogs relax and feeling at home and she knew exactly how a westie should be cut. Over the years we became good friends with Lynn and her husband Ron. Their help over the years has been very much appreciated and we often joked that Lynn was Hamish's personal assistant and Ron was the camera man snapping Hamish at every opportunity.

As we have never had a dog before we thought it would be a good idea to attend puppy training classes. Having found a course in a local church hall we set off to enrol and joked that we probably needed training as well. When we arrived I guess there were about twenty puppies in the hall which turned out initially to be chaotic with all the puppies playing together and helpers mobbing up behind them. Proceedings were soon brought to order and the trainer introduced herself to all the owners. She was a very upright lady with a forceful voice and asked us first to parade in a circle with our puppies on their leads so she could access our ability. We then proceeded to get a very firm lecture on how badly we all did and told in no uncertain terms they was a lot of hard work required to get our training certificate. At least it was an honest assessment and we were all determined to do well.

All seemed to be going well and Margaret was getting to grips with the training. However, one particular activity involved getting your puppy to sit, then command them to wait off the lead, walk four paces away and then calling the dog to you with the reward of a treat. Back home I had a plan where I could shine at our next training class by getting Hamish to sit by my side and then walk several paces before calling him. I progressively walked further away from Hamish and was now ready to impress the trainer at our next class. Tuesday night duly arrived and I thought I was going to be top of the class. When my turn came I turned to face Hamish, made him sit of the lead and then proceeded to walk right across the hall.

As I turned to face Hamish a voice bellowed *"What are you doing Mr Crossby"*. Oh dear I was then told in no uncertain terms that I was to do as instructed and not what I wanted to do. That evening I left with my tail between my legs!

Chapter Seven –
Pets As Therapy

Back home after our Isle of Wight holiday we quickly got back in our routine which was of course revolved around Hamish. Know that Hamish was now house trained Hamish had the run of the house and invariably when Margaret returned from her part time work Hamish was sitting on the settee looking out the window in anticipation of his lunch. We asked our neighbours if they had heard Hamish while Margaret was at work but they both replied that he had not barked which we took to be a good sign that he was not distressed while Margaret was out. Margaret would feed Hamish one of his meals at lunchtime and then take him over the park for his daily exercise.

One thing Hamish also enjoyed was going to Margaret's allotment in the evenings where he would invariably pick up a foxes scent. It was nice to see his true terrier instincts coming out and these were happy times for him on warm summer's evenings.

Not forgetting how moved we had been by the TV appeal we had seen for Pets As Therapy we contacted our local hospital's Volunteer Services Department to see if we could become Pets as Therapy volunteers. By coincidence the Volunteer Manager was already thinking about introducing a PAT Dog scheme into the hospital and advised us to speak direct to the Charity to find out what was required to get registered as a visiting PAT Dog.

The PAT website was very helpful and we found out that Hamish would have to pass a test first which would be carried out by the local Pat Co-ordinator.

The test consisted of a number of individual items *e.g.* *"What was the first impression of the dog?"* the examiner would be looking for a calm dog that did not jump up. *"When offering a treat how did the dog react?"* The examiner would expect the dog to sit and wait. *"How did the dog react to making a sudden noise?"* The examiner would expect the dog not to react to noise and bark. For the next two weeks we practiced with Hamish so he was familiar with the test he would get and we hoped he would pass the test first time.

We now thought the time was right for Hamish to have the test and I made a phone call to our local Pat Co-ordinator. The lady named Patricia lived very local to us about six miles away and she was very helpful but did stress that Hamish was still very young and in her experience it was rare for a young westie to pass the test first time. Whilst I understood the reason for this we both knew Hamish was extremely calm and felt confident he would stand a good chance of passing.

Patricia was however still happy to meet Hamish and carry out the test and she asked what bus she should catch to get to our property. I then had what I thought would be a good idea and said I was happy to provide a lift in our car which I hoped would get us off on the right foot.

So as to make a good impression I collected Patricia at precisely the agreed time. Patricia had a very nice demeanour and was smartly dressed in a two piece outfit and after our introductions we set off for home. On the way we chatted about Hamish and how we were moved by the television appeal we had watched on the Isle of Wight.

As we approached our house I said it was likely that Hamish would be waiting at the window and sure enough as we parked there was Hamish patiently waiting.

Armed with her clip board I opened the front door and Hamish came bounding up the hall. I instructed Hamish to sit in a firm voice and fortunately he obeyed my command. Patricia gave Hamish a stroke and this seemed to go well and hopefully a tick on the test paper. Hamish was his usual calm self and he even ignored the noise test when Patricia dropped her clip board on the floor which made a loud noise.

The final test was to see Hamish walking on a short lead so we set off to our local park. After completing two laps of the park we returned home for tea and cake and hopefully the result of the test. It felt like we were both back at school waiting the results of examination and my heart rate had certainly increased.

We both hoped Hamish had done enough to pass and to our amazement Patricia announced he had passed with flying colours. She went on to say that considering the young age of Hamish she was expecting him to fail but had to admit he was one of the most laid back westies she had ever meet. I of course took Patricia back home and said we would stay in touch and let her know how our first visit to the hospital went.

Chapter Eight –
Hospital Visiting

It took quite some time for it to sink in that Hamish had passed his Pat Dog test and we couldn't wait to tell Hamish's breeder Brenda the good news. Brenda was excited to receive the good news and kindly asked if we would like to visit her and have Sunday lunch. A date was set and we were looking forward to letting Brenda see Hamish now he was over a year old and what a beautiful Westie he had become. Not only in looks but his nature and without doubt Brenda had chosen the right Westie for us from the litter.

It was so nice to re-visit Brenda and her husband Clifford and they wanted to know all about what Hamish had been doing for the past year and they were so pleased that Hamish was going to be a Pets As Therapy dog and visit people in our local hospital. We wondered if Hamish would remember the surroundings he was raised in as a puppy but seemed to be more interested in the joint of beef that Clifford had prepared. It was a hearty lunch and it was so nice to talk to Brenda again as we both realised we were so lucky to find such a good breeder.

Back home again our lives continued as normal and we thought it would be a good idea to contact our local hospital to check that they were still happy for Hamish to visit. The Volunteer Services Manager was as excited as us to receive the news that Hamish had passed his PAT dog test and she said she would speak to the ward sister of elderly care to agree a date for our first visit. The hospital also had to check with the Infection Control Doctor and

Consultant Microbiologist to confirm that dogs presented no risk of infection to patients, relatives and staff.

All we could do now was to patiently wait for our certificate to arrive together with the PAT dog jacket and lead. By the end of February 2001 everything was in place and the Volunteer Manager had also arranged for our local newspapers the Croydon Advertiser and Croydon Guardian to attend our first visit. This was brilliant news as it would provide valuable publicity for our Charity and generally raise awareness of what animal can achieve in bringing comfort to patients in hospitals.

It was both an exciting and defining moment for us and we were so proud of Hamish and what he had achieved in a short space of time. We were confident that with his loving nature patients would fall in love with him. The day of our first hospital visit finally arrived and we assembled first in the Volunteer Managers office who explained that the local newspapers would take pictures on the ward. The ward sister also explained that following the afternoon rest period she would open the ward doors and switch on the lights. Being an old Victorian ward the ward sister informed us that the beds were set out in single rows and not the modern idea of separate bays.

Hamish looked very smart in his uniform and our groomer Lynn had given Hamish a bath and trim and he was ready to start this new experience. Before we could get nervous the ward lights came on and all the patients were all staring at Hamish with what I can only describe as a look of surprise. This very quickly turned to smiles and all the patients wanted to stroke Hamish and make a fuss of him and they told us stories of animals they had in the past and how pleased they were to see a dog in the hospital.

The ward sister commented *"The opportunity for patients to stroke and cuddle Hamish should help to motivate and relax patients and might even increase their recovery rate"*. I think the Croydon Advertiser summed up the feeling of the day with their newspaper headline *"Hamish just the tonic as he visits sick in Mayday Hospital"*.

We were so proud of Hamish that day and he just took it all in his stride, nothing seemed to faze him which was amazing considering he was still only 18 months old!

As a part of our weekly visits to the hospital we had a request to visit the stroke ward as the Physiotherapists wanted to gauge the reaction of patients seeing Hamish. It is quite common that sick patients do not react to human contact but it is very different with an animal that is non judgemental. At times it was amazing to see a patient who had lost the use of their hands due to a stroke would try and move their hands to touch Hamish.

With every week that past we were all gaining in confidence and Hamish walked around as if he had been born to be a Pat dog. We quickly realised that it was not only the patients who wanted to see Hamish but the staff and relatives were also pleased to see him and commented that Hamish was a ray of sunshine and made their stressful day a little easier.

Looking back it is impossible to say how many patients Hamish had seen over the years but some patients left us with lasting memories that will be with us for the rest of our lives.

Not everybody can appreciate or understand the connection an animal can have with sick patients but I think the following two stories sum up that bond.

We were asked to visit a patient named John who had suffered a very severe stroke and was not able to get out of bed. John was an animal lover and when he met Hamish he instantly fell in love with him and described Hamish as *"his special company"*. We continued to visit John for several weeks and his wife even told us that he had to see Hamish first before any other visitors on the days we visited John. We built up such a rapport with John seeing him enjoying the company of Hamish. John's wife had told us that he was going to be transferred to a specialist nursing home as she would not be able to look after John at home anymore. It was very sad to receive that news but realised that John needed special care. We missed seeing John and knew he would be missing Hamish. By coincidence several months later we bumped into John's wife who gave us the sad news that John had passed away. She went on to say that the family had put a picture of Hamish in John's coffin and hoped we did not mind. We both agreed later that Hamish had been there for John and had brought him so much joy into his life as his *"special company"*, words we will always remember.

On the stroke ward we meet a family whose mother was in a coma and as she liked dogs asked us to make a visit to see if it would aid their mother's recovery. We were informed that when a person is in a coma their brain can still be active.

For several weeks we used to visit the comatosed lady and speak to her saying Hamish was here to visit her. We hoped it would aid her recovery and to our surprise the family approached us before our next visit saying that Mum had woken up and the first words she said were *"where is Hamish"* It was so nice to see her sitting up in bed and she was able to give Hamish a big cuddle.

By this time the hospital staff agreed that Hamish was making a real difference to people's lives and was given the nickname of *"The 4 legged medicine"*.

On one occasion we were visiting one of the elderly care wards and spoke to a lady whose face we recognised. She was so pleased to see Hamish and revealed to us that in her earlier life she had been a dancer and singer. She went on to say that she auditioned for the Australian actor Barry Humphries who had invented the character Dame Edna Everage. We then remembered that the lady was named Madge on the TV show and was hired to be a stooge for Barry Humphries character as the person who never smiled in his company. We were so pleased to have met her and both agreed that it had taken a dog to make Madge smile!

We were also beginning to realise that not all patients liked dog and didn't want to see Hamish. Margaret used to go on ahead of me in the wards and ask if they wanted to stroke Hamish or give him a cuddle. On one elderly care ward a lady looked up and said rather loudly *"is that a dog"* Margaret quickly replied *"No they have just changed your medication"*. Where patients didn't want a visit I used to just hold Hamish up and in the main we always got a smile.

It must be Wednesday

Hamish starting his ward rounds

Meeting Hospital patients

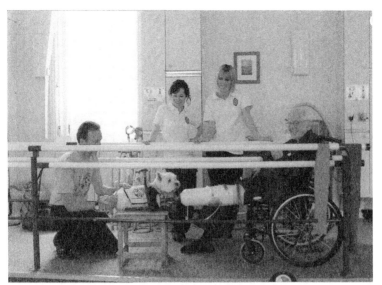

Hamish at work

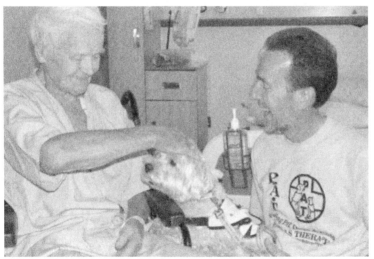

Above big smile

Above Hamish receiving his 10 year hospital volunteering certificate

Below Hamish with other hospital volunteers

Chapter Nine-
Promoting Pets as Therapy

Away from hospital visiting we wanted to get involved in raising awareness of the Pets as Therapy charity and decided to help our local co-ordinator with PAT talks. There were plenty of opportunities for talks at Women's Institutes, Church and Resident's Association groups and one thing quickly came to light that very few people we spoke to were not aware of the work the charity does everyday throughout the UK. I used to start my presentation with the question *"how many people present had heard of our charity"*. The number was always very small but at least our presence was getting the message across. We enjoyed going to these evening meetings but of course most people just wanted to see Hamish and the other Pat dogs we took with us. However, I think the highlight of the meetings for Hamish was when the refreshments were served in the interval as he knew a treat would be forthcoming!

During the summer months we attended various road shows and our stand was always busy with people wanting to know more about the charity and taking the opportunity to make a fuss of the Pat dogs present.

One area of work which Hamish excelled at was visiting phobic children and this was especially close to my heart as I was nervous of dogs from a very young age. One example of where Hamish was a great help was being asked by our charity to visit a Children's Centre in Croydon to help a young girl get over her phobia of being near a dog and our brief was to try to get the girl to be confident to hold Hamish's lead and take him for a walk.

Hamish had the reputation of being the "starter dog" as being small and very appealing he didn't portray being a threat. We spoke to the girl's mum first and said our plan was to start by just introducing Hamish and keeping him on his lead. We meet up on a regular basis and slowly the girl's confidence started to improve as she was developing a bond with Hamish. After the eighth visit the girl was able to hold the lead and take him for a short walk. At no time did Hamish bark or pull on his lead and we are sure he sensed he was there to help. Our part of the therapy was complete and the next step was the introduction of a larger dog to continue on from the groundwork we had started. A few months later we meet the family in our local park and to our surprise the girl had her own dog. We were over the moon to see this and so proud that Hamish had been involved in helping the girl get over her phobia.

Another request we had was for us to visit a girl named Jodie who had learning difficulties and resided in a specialist home. We were told she was terrified of dogs and home wasn't able to take Jodie outside of the home for walks or visits. When we arrived at the home we had a meeting with the occupational therapist who thought the best approach initially was for us to stand in the car park adjacent to the entrance and introduce Hamish from a distance in the knowledge she was in a safe space. To communicate we would use our mobile phones. We didn't achieve very much on our first visit but at least Jodie was able to look at Hamish through a window and the therapist explained to her that Hamish was a very special dog and he would like to come into the home for a visit

The following week Jodie was able to stand in the open doorway and again we just held Hamish on his lead so Jodie could see he was calm. Jodie seemed to be gaining in confidence and on our next visit we were able to take Hamish into the Home albeit at a safe distance. After another few visits Jodie was then able to hold Hamish's lead and walk him around the car park. We heard several weeks later that Jodie was now able to leave the home without any fear that she was going to be attacked by a dog and all this was down to the calmness of Hamish and we were so pleased that Hamish was able to help Jodie.

To improve awareness of our charity and spread the word what a wonderful job PAT dogs and their owners do day in and day out we also volunteered to take part in a ring display at Discover Dogs which used to be held at Earls Court in London. On the day of the event we meet up at our stand and told that we would be parading around the ring and then visitors would be given the opportunity to meet the Pat dogs. This was a brilliant way to spread the message to the public and Hamish as usual took it all in his stride and enjoyed the attention he was getting.

Above Hamish with Pets As Therapy volunteers collecting
for the Charity
Below Hamish on a road show in Grangewood Park
Croydon

Chapter Ten –
Other Work

My work colleagues at Croydon Council were aware of the work Hamish was doing as a registered Pat dog and the Road Safety Section had the idea of using Hamish as a mascot for the Junior Road Safety Club. The road safety scheme was promoted by Transport for London to engage children of Junior School age and get them to run clubs within their respective schools and pass road safety messages to their class mates. Hamish quickly gained the title of "Junior Canine Road Safety Officer" and attended school assemblies where invited. A magazine was also published every three months and Hamish had his own articles on providing helpful tips for the children when they were out and about. As Hamish used to wear his Pat dog jacket it was decided to run a competition in all Croydon schools to design a road safety jacket especially for him. Some of the children came up with brilliant ideas for the wording on the jacket but the winning slogan was *"paws before you cross the road"*.

To reward all the members of the road safety club an annual event was held in the Fairfields Hall where certificates and badges were presented to the children. Hamish of course was one of the guests of honour and he also received his certificate and badge. Another guest of honour that supported the event was the late David Prowes who was the Green Cross Code man in the television adverts and or course the legendry Darth Vader in the star wars films.

Above Hamish with winner of the jacket for his road safety work
Below Hamish modelling his new road safety jacket

Hamish helping out at a road safety event

Hamish with the Smart Brothers

Hamish with members of the junior road safety club 2008

Hamish Mc Fee
CROYDON'S "CANINE" ROAD SAFETY OFFICER

Hamish Mc Fee joined us in July 2008 as a Canine JRSO. He proved himself worthy of this title by demonstrating how to cross the road safely with his handler, using the six rules of the green cross code.

Hamish may be able to visit your school if you are having a special Road Safety day or Road Safety assembly.

Contact
susan.m

Hamish Mc Fee
Was presented with his CJRSO jacket, badge and certificate at the Town Hall by the Mayor of Croydon.

Croydon's JRSO's are invited to

this special presentation day every year in recognition of their hard work promoting Road Safety.

Hamish Mcfee

Every year Croydon Council hold an award ceremony to recognise and celebrate the hard work, commitment, dedication and achievement of staff and volunteers.

It was a black tie event and Hamish received an invitation to attend including a gala dinner. Hamish wore his road safety jacket complete with a very smart tartan bowtie. As usual Hamish was a credit to us and everybody we meet just wanted to hear about what he had achieved and the work he did as mascot for the Junior Road Safety Club. To our surprise Hamish was invited onto the stage to receive a highly commended award and it was announced to the audience that he participated in road safety demonstrations at Schools across the borough encouraging children to develop good road sense.

Hamish with Barry and Margaret

Chapter Eleven –
Returning to the Isle of Wight

We returned many times to the Isle of Wight for holidays with Hamish staying at various cottages and every time we said wouldn't it be brilliant if one day we could buy a small bolt hole on the Island. That opportunity arose in 2008 when I was able to take the lump sum from my Council pension which enabled us to buy a one bedroom cottage. Our friend Jim kindly said we could stay with him for a few days so we drew up a short list of properties to view. We all set off to view the properties but at the end of the day we hadn't found anything that appealed to us and that would be suitable for Hamish. Talking it over with Jim later we realised that the properties we were viewing didn't give us that holiday feeling. I then remembered seeing a one bedroom villa being advertised on Rightmove which was adjacent to Wootton Creek, located in a holiday village, and we decided to visit the property in the hope it would be suitable. As soon as we drove past the Creek we immediately realised that this location gave us the holiday feeling we wanted but the property being advertised was in need of refurbishment which our budget would not stretch to. We returned back to the mainland feeling disappointed but at least knowing where we would like to but a property on the Island.

We soon got into our routine with Hamish back home and decided to just wait and see if another property came up for sale. I continued to monitor the property market and found that a villa on the estate was being sold at auction.

That night I asked our friend Jim if he would go and view the property from the outside and let us know if it was worth pursuing. He phoned back later in the evening saying it looked in very good condition and we should arrange to view it before the auction.

Within the next few days we had arranged a viewing and set off again to the Isle of Wight for a day trip to view the property. As Jim had said it was in good condition and we made the decision to attend the auction in Southampton. Jim kindly said we could stay with him again and so off we set again for a few days. We are not sure what Hamish thought about all this travelling but like always he just took it all in his stride. The property auction was quite intense and when our auction lot arrived my head was just spinning and before we knew it the auctioneers hammer came down and we had bought a property on the Isle of Wight.

Hamish always enjoyed going to the Isle of Wight and it was becoming his second home and somewhere he could chill out and have a well earnt break from his Pat dog duties.

We stumbled across a pub in the village of Havenstreet and used to have a meal there. The owners were very friendly and loved to see Hamish. I think he quickly got to know that if he sat patiently he would be rewarded with a treat. We had a favourite corner table where Hamish could lie on the floor under the bench seat which I guess was like a cave to him. On one of our visits to the pub we were both enjoying our meal when we noticed one of the waitresses coming towards us holding a westie by the lead. I thought to myself that it was the spitting image of Hamish and then realised it was Hamish who was found walking around the bar area.

Chapter Twelve –
The Croydon Guardian

We now had a very rigid weekly routine with Hamish visiting Croydon University Hospital's stroke and elderly care wards and it was proving to be a big hit with the patients, relatives and staff. It was brought to our attention by a member of staff that the Croydon Guardian were looking for nominations for its annual Croydon Champions Awards and they felt that we should apply on behalf of Hamish as he deserved to be nominated. We kept thinking about these awards and decided to make an online application explaining what Hamish was achieving with his hospital visiting.

To our surprise a few weeks later we received a phone call from the paper saying that Hamish had been shortlisted in the category of Community Champion and they would like to come to our house to take a picture for inclusion in the paper. At least another month went by without any news when a letter arrived from the newspaper with an invitation to attend the award ceremony in a new hall adjoining the Selsdon Library in Croydon.

It was a very exciting evening and on arrival in the foyer area there were electronic message boards with one being dedicated to Hamish showing pictures of him in the Hospital. A buffet was then served before sitting down in the main hall for the presentation of the awards. On this occasion Hamish didn't win in his category but as a runner up he was still invited onto the stage to rapturous applause from the audience. In my excitement I dropped Hamish's lead which resulted in everybody on the stage including the Croydon mayor trying to round him up.

To our surprise a headline in the following week's Guardian reported that Hamish did not win but he *"stole the show"*. We then got a phone call from the newspaper asking if Hamish would become their mascot for future years which we were honoured to accept. Every year we then supported the Croydon Guardian with the launch of their Champions Awards in various outside locations around Croydon. We remember one year arriving in our main shopping mall where the Newspaper's stand was set up but was not achieving any interest from the public. We thought of a solution by sitting Hamish on the centre of the stand and within minute's people started to gather. His cuteness had won the day again and the following week the Newspaper reported the launch of the awards with the headline *"Hamish attracts a Crowd"*. This headline summed up the appeal of Hamish and his ability to make a difference to people's lives and we both agreed long may it last.

Hamish meeting a young fan in the Whitgift Centre
Croydon

Chapter Thirteen –
Pat Dog of the Year Award
2009/10

Every year the Pets as Therapy Charity ask for nominations from owners of their PAT dogs to be considered for the prestigious award of PAT dog of the year which was sponsored by the Yours Magazine, Hi Life Dog Food and the RSPCA. After getting a runners up award as a community champion from our local newspaper in 2004 we decided to nominate Hamish but up to 2009 we never managed to get short listed. With over 4,500 registered Pat Dogs at that time and all deserving to win it was going to be very difficult to get short listed?

In conjunction with submitting a photograph of Hamish it was a requirement to give a written statement of how your Pat dog had made a difference to someone's life. We thought about this for some considerable time and remembered how Hamish had visited the lady in a coma and when she woke up saying the words *"Where's Hamish"* seemed to be the perfect example of how he had made a difference to someone's life.

We duly submitted Hamish's details and then put it to the back of our minds as we needed to focus on taking Hamish to the hospital so he could continue with his Pat dog duties. The word soon got around the hospital that we had put Hamish forward for entry into the PAT dog of the year awards and everybody we meet said they would vote for Hamish if he was short listed.

The closing date for entries came and went and we thought Hamish was not going to be in the final six when a letter arrived in the post with the good news that Hamish had been short listed.

Life after that seemed to go into overdrive and our excitement was mounting that Hamish would be at Crufts in the main arena. To enable the public to choose their favourite dog we had a visit from the Yours Magazine and a photograph was taken of Hamish which featured in the October 2009 edition of the magazine along with the other five finalists. The eventual winner would be decided by the readers of the magazine and the celebrity patrons which included the late Roy Hudd and the celebrity chef James Martin. Prior to going to Crufts we were informed by Pets as Therapy that we would also have to attend a one day training course at a dog training centre near Oxford. The running time of the arena display would be half an hour which would culminate in the presentation of the Pat Dog of the year award.

It was a chilly day in November when we set off for training centre and as usual Hamish took the journey in his stride . He was a very good traveller in the car and had the ability to sleep most of the journey but always seemed to know when we arrived as his head would pop up eager to find out where we were. The indoor training area was very small and with twenty Pat dogs in the display we were told that part of the day would be spent in a field outside which was roughly the size of the Crufts Main Arena. After listening to the running order of our show we were told that the last ten minutes would be devoted to the presentation and each finalist would be called in turn to stand under the spot light in the main arena and each individual story would be read out to the audience. Once back in line the countdown to the winner would then be announced and the presentation party including the late Roy Barraclough would enter the arena.

We must have spent about two hours outside in the field practicing the running order of our presentation and at the end of it we were all extremely cold and glad we could go back inside for a welcome cup of tea. Before leaving for home we were told that we would have to go to Crufts for two days and we should all book accommodation near to the NEC. Our entry passes and further instruction would arrive after Christmas in the post and in the meant time we should encourage people to go online and vote for their favourite PAT dog. Overall all the finalists deserved to win and we were just grateful that we had made the final six and whatever the outcome it was going to be a wonderful experience being at Crufts in the main arena.

It was a tradition in the hospital for some of the volunteers to go around the wards carol singing in the weeks leading up to Christmas and we thought it would be a good idea for Hamish to air his vocal chords and join in. While the volunteers were singing carols in the wards we would take Hamish around to the individual beds and wish the patients a very happy Christmas. This was a great success and the evening ended with all of us assembling in the hospital chapel for mince pies and mulled wine. Hamish of course had his own doggy treats to enjoy. In recognition of the hard work carried out by volunteers we were also all treated to a Christmas lunch which included some form of entertainment. The Croydon Mayor used to attend as well and in their speech to the volunteers Hamish always got a mention. In fact over the years Hamish meet twelve different Mayors and as you will read later on he even had a one to one visit with the Mayor in his parlour. An honour indeed!

Hamish always enjoyed the Christmas period as he liked having his human family around him and of course it meant there would be some presents with toys or treats inside.

Hamish was never particularly interested in toys and got bored with them very quickly usually when the toy stopped squeaking. He did, however, like his treat ball and if you put a treat inside the ball he would nudge it around the room until it popped out. So as not to over feed Hamish with treats we used to keep back some of his kibble to use in the treat ball and he was none the wiser.

After Christmas we resumed our PAT dog visits to the hospital and everybody we meet both staff and relatives said they would vote for Hamish in the up and coming PAT dog of the year event at Crufts. January and February flew by and before we knew it we were on our way to the NEC in Birmingham having already secured our hotel accommodation in a hotel right next to the exhibition centre.

For those of you that have never been to Crufts it is an amazing experience with the halls jammed packed with stands, holding areas and side rings all surrounding the Main Arena. It's hard to describe the buss and constant sounds from all the excited dogs but an experience you will not forget. Of course Hamish just took it all in his stride and we were asked to report to our holding area two hours before our appearance in the main ring. To keep Hamish safe from all the passing foot traffic we wheeled Hamish around on a porter's trolley sitting on our cool bag which provided an ideal seat. This novel idea was a big hit with all the visitors and they all smiled as we went by.

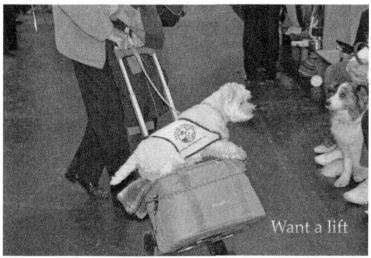

Hamish taking a rest at Crufts

A lot of people stopped us and wanted to know more about the Pets as Therapy charity and enabled us to direct them to our stand to get more information and hopefully make a much needed donation.

The morning just flew by and we meet up with the other finalists and other PAT Dogs in the display at our holding area so we could all walk to the main arena together. W could tell that nerves were kicking in and we were told to just relax and enjoy the experience of being in the most famous dog arena in the world. Just before we were due to enter the main arena the presentation party assembled which included the late Roy Barrowclough who was going to present the award to the winner. There was no more time to get nervous as the music started up and we all filed in to commence our presentation.

You see the main arena on the television but when you are actually inside the arena it is huge and it is exhilarating with all the buzz from the audience and the lighting.

We paraded around the arena and then came to a halt just like we rehearsed. The public were given the facts about the charity and where all the Pat dogs in the ring visited. I must admit it was hard to concentrate wondering if Hamish would be awarded the ultimate award of Pat Dog of the Year. Each of the shortlisted PAT dogs including Hamish went into the centre of the arena under the spotlight where their individual stories were read out. It seemed quite surreal to see Hamish on the giant video screens and thought to myself whatever the outcome we had made it into the final of the competition and in truth all six finalists deserved to win.

To add to the suspense of the occasion the results were called out in reverse order 6th place ..... 5th place ..... 4th place ..... 3rd place

I suddenly realised that Hamish's name had not been called and we were in the final two. 2nd place was then announced and again it was not Hamish! Before I could gather my thoughts the announcer said *"And the winner of the 2009/10 Pets as Therapy Dog of the Year is Hamish McFee"*. We had won and the clapping from the audience was deafening. The presentation party then entered the ring and cameras were flashing everywhere. Margaret, who had been carrying a banner around the arena, joined me and the late Roy Barrowclough presented our award before we did a lap of honour around the ring. We were so pleased that our friends Lynn and Ron were in the audience cheering us on and were able to witness Hamish winning first hand.

Looking back on this achievement people often ask us how we felt at the time. It's hard to express in words what was running through our minds but it was a mixture of pent up emotion and a feeling of not believing Hamish's name had been called out as the winner. Standing in the main arena of the world's most famous dog show and having your dog's name called out was just mind blowing and something we will always remember.

As for Hamish he was as calm as a cucumber and just posed for photographs from the waiting reporters. Back at the PAT Stand we had several interviews with reporters who all wanted our story.

What a day it had been and Hamish had won the ultimate award of Pat Dog of the Year. Our heads by now were just spinning thinking about what Hamish had achieved. Back home we did more interviews with our local paper. Going to Crufts is both exhausting and exhilarating and an experience we both will never forget.

Hamish with the late Roy Barraclough at Crufts

Above Hamish being presented with his award as Pat Dog
of the Year 2010

Below Hamish getting a cuddle from the late
Roy Barraclough at Crufts

Chapter Fourteen – Croydon Guardian Champions 2010

Hamish continued to attend the annual Croydon Champions Awards in his role as their mascot which gave us the opportunity to promote the work that Pets as Therapy does in the UK. Hamish as of course always the centre of attraction at the awards ceremony and Hamish's trimmer Lynn who was also very good at compiling DVD's of the work Hamish was doing used to produce a short three minute DVD which was shown before the first half interval. This proved very popular and always got a very loud round of applause from the invited audience.

After entering Hamish in the category of Community Champion in 2004 we thought we should put his name forward again in 2010 in the hope that he may win at the second go. My mind immediately went back to the award ceremony in 2004 and I thought to myself if he does win and we go on stage I must keep hold of his lead this time and not end up chasing him around the stage again!

It was another full on event with a school orchestra playing to invited guests until it was time to take our seats for the main event of presenting the awards in the various categories. The tension was mounting as the nominations in Hamish's category were announced and to our surprise Hamish's name was read out as the winner. Yet another award to add to Hamish's collection and we wondered to ourselves what was going to be the next award?

Hamish as usual took everything in his stride but one incident did take us by surprise. Margaret had to have an operation and due to the long waiting list she decided to have the procedure privately

The operation was a complete success and Margaret had told the nurses looking after her about the work Hamish was doing and permission was given for Hamish to make a visit. All the staff were so pleased to see Hamish and I was expecting him to be excited when he saw Margaret in her hospital bed. However, I was not expecting the reaction we got from Hamish as he was clearly disturbed when he saw Margaret in bed and wouldn't even look at her. So as not to distress him any further I decided to take him home and driving back in the car I was trying to understand what the problem was when it dawned on me that Hamish was not used to seeing Margaret in a hospital bed and clearly this had worried him. I guess we should have realised this could happen and Hamish was so happy when Margaret came home that for days he would follow her everywhere.

Dogtor Mc Fee

Chapter Fifteen – Daily Mirror Animal Hero Awards

With all the commitments we had with Hamish he was of course our beloved family pet and in every respect he was a Westie through and through. He loved being with us and just being a normal dog. I remember one occasion when we were in bed listening to the early morning sounds of the milkman coming up our road. Hamish was asleep in his bed in the corner of the bedroom when all of a sudden he rushed to the window and started barking. Due to the height of the window Hamish could not see out but something was clearly disturbing him. I quickly jumped out of bed to calm Hamish down and looking out of the window I realised why he was barking. "It was a different milkman" and to this day we still don't understand how Hamish knew it was a different milkman and it remains one of life's mysteries!

Margaret is an avid reader of the Daily Mirror and she noticed that the paper was going to hold an Animal Hero Awards event similar to the Pride of Britain Awards. The awards would honour the outstanding achievements of animals in the UK. It was going to be a star studded event taking place in a London Hotel and Amanda Holden would be hosting the awards ceremony.

We didn't think for one minute Hamish would be shortlisted but we decided to apply as Hamish and completed an online application briefly setting out what Hamish had achieved as a PAT Dog and relayed the story of Hamish visiting the lady in a coma.

Several weeks later we received a call from the Daily Mirror stating that Hamish had made the final three in the category of Caring Animal of the Year and we would be invited to attend the Langham Hotel in London for the presentation of the award. We were able to take two guests with us so we invited our good friends Lynn and Ron to join us and we all decided to get a taxi to make the journey easier for Hamish. On arrival we walked up the red carpet and felt like Hollywood Celebrities with the flashing of cameras and cheering from the waiting crowd.

Once inside there was a welcome reception where the invited celebrities mingled with us eager to find out what Hamish did in his role as a Pets as Therapy dog. Some of the celebrities we meet that night included Brian May from the rock band Queen with his wife Anita Dobson, Bill Oddy and Debra Meadon. Debra in particular was very interested in the work Hamish was doing.

Before the awards ceremony took place we all sat down to a three course meal and Hamish just laid quietly under our table oblivious to all the noise and chatter surrounding us. All through the meal you could feel the tension rising when Amanda Holden appeared on stage and introduced the ceremony and summed it up by saying "We'd like to say congratulations to all our winners, you have shown immense courage and kindness, you've sacrificed so others could have, you've gone beyond the call of duty time and time again, you've cared when others wouldn't, you've not wanted praise or sought it".

It was certainly said from the heart but to us it was a pleasure to bring some happiness and joy to others, especially those who feel isolated and lonely in hospital.

The winner of our category was first to be announced and Amanda ran through the three finalists and clearly Hamish was up against strong competition from a retired police horse and Labrador Lucy who was a guide dog for the blind buddy programme. Any of us deserved to be the winner and before we could catch our breath Hamish was announced as the winner and we were invited to the stage to receive our award from the late Sara Harding from Girl's Aloud. We then were ushered back stage for a formal photo shoot. Sara wanted to know all about the work Hamish did and we found out that she had dogs of her own. There were some truly amazing stories that night and we were so proud of Hamish to have been called an animal hero. During the interval McFly provided the entertainment and speaking to them back stage they joked that they should make a record named Hamish McFly.

It was indeed a star studded five star event that we live in our memories for ever and on the way home we just couldn't stop talking about it. We later received a letter from Gavin Grant who was the RSPCA Chief Executive and it read:-

"I am writing to congratulate you for winning a well deserved award at last week's inaugural RSPCA Daily Mirror Animal Hero Awards. I am sure you will agree it was a wonderful celebration of true heroism shown by animals and human beings, made even more so by hearing stories like yours.

What a remarkable range of outstanding bravery and dedication we saw. As owners of twelve year old Hamish you must be incredibly proud of his achievements. Hamish's exceptional bedside manner is both moving and inspirational, he has clearly made a lasting impression and touched a lot of people's lives.

The joy and comfort Hamish's larger than life company brings is a therapy like no other. Your storey allowed us to celebrate the best in humanity that is only stimulated by the love for our fellow creatures"

We have framed this letter and the wording just encapsulates what Pets as Therapy is all about. The memory of that wonderful night will live on in our memories forever.

Animal Hero Awards 2013 the winning party

Above Hamish meeting the late Sara Harding

Hamish McFee...Winner...Daily Mirror & RSPCA Animal Hero Award 2013

Chapter Sixteen - Hospital Outings and more

Every year the hospital Volunteer manager arranged a summer outing, usually to the coast, as a thank you for all the volunteers work in the hospital throughout the year.

It became a tradition that the Croydon mayor would speak to the volunteers and wave the coaches off. This gave us the opportunity for Hamish to have his photo taken with the Mayor and throughout his life he met twelve Mayors. One mayor in particular Jonathan Driver unfortunately died in Office but we have fond memories of his support of the work Hamish did and on the occasions we met him he always said in a broad Yorkshire accent *"Ello Amish"*. He unfortunately could not attend the volunteer's summer outing send off and to make up for this Hamish had a personal invitation to visit the Mayor in his Chamber for a photo shoot which was very much appreciated. A very special man who is sadly missed by all that knew him.

Hamish with the late Jonathan Driver taken in the Mayor's Parlour

61

One incident that stick in our mind during one of our outings still makes us laugh as it nearly caused a riot when the volunteers were boarding the coach when the coach driver said *"that dog is not coming on my coach"*. Oh dear we thought that's the end of our summer outing at which point all the volunteers that had boarded the coach said together *"if Hamish doesn't go we won't either"*. The volunteer Manager then explained to the driver that it had been cleared by the coach company that Hamish could go on the coach at which point we boarded to a hearty round of applause. People power wins again!

Hamish's send off at a volunteers outing

Chapter Seventeen–
Later Life

As Hamish began to slow down in later life we started to make adjustments to our hospital visiting as Hamish was still eager to continue his hospital visits but we were very mindful that we had to scale back the work he was doing both inside the hospital and outside. With this in mind we decided to concentrate on visiting the stroke ward and only visit other wards where a special request for a visit had been forthcoming.

Health wise Hamish had been a very healthy dog overall but we noticed that his eyes were starting to glaze over. Our vet referred us to an eye specialist and we were told that Hamish was developing cataracts in both his eyes. Fortunately Hamish adjusted very well and this impediment didn't seem to affect him in any way. Hearing like any other aging dog also become a problem but in some ways like the sounds of fireworks did not frighten him anymore. For years we always dreaded firework night and we tried to work out why Hamish didn't cope well with fireworks. We racked our brains and eventually put it down to the afternoon we first collected Hamish. On the way home we went through a violent storm with thunder and lighting and having just left his familiar surrounding may account for his fear of loud bangs.

On other thing Hamish did not like was aggression and this was highlighted on one of our spring breaks when we visited West bay in Dorset. Hamish loved the beach and in particular the rocks around West Bay where he would spend endless hours exploring.

On one occasion we were having a rest on the beach watching a dad playing with his young children who were shouting out loud with excitement when all of a sudden Hamish ran up to the dad and started barking. We quickly went in pursuit of Hamish and suddenly realised what the problem was. Hamish of course thought the dad was hurting the children and he was trying to intervene to stop it. We apologised to the family and explained that Hamish was very sensitive and was only trying to protect the children. They fully understood and we went on to tell the family all about his Pets as Therapy work.

As all dog owners will confirm time seems to accelerate when your beloved pets gets older and we knew all too well that we would eventually have to make the decision to retire Hamish. It was going to be a hard decision to make but his well being had to come first. As it turned out we did not have to make this decision as the worst weekend of our live was rapidly approaching when we would lose our beloved Hamish Mc Fee.

6TH JANUARY...16TH BIRTHDAY TODAY AND STILL MAKING PEOPLE HAPPY

Chapter Eighteen– Losing Hamish

It was a truly beautiful spring day in April 2017 and the weekend started like any other by walking Hamish in our local park. I always meet up with other dog walkers but as Hamish was slowing down they used to go ahead and catch us up on the second lap. Hamish still enjoyed his park walks and spent most of the time sniffing trees and clumps of grass. The rest of the day passed without anything unforeseen happening and we settled down in the evening as usual to catch up on some TV programmes. Hamish would stretch out on the settee and all was good with the world.

Margaret went off to bed about 10pm and I decided to make a cup of tea before going to bed as well. As it turned out I never got to finish the tea as all of a sudden Hamish became very restless and I assumed he just wanted to go into the garden. Hamish must have been in the garden for a good 10 minutes before coming in and then about 5 minutes later he wanted to go back into the garden again. I thought nothing of this at the time and decided to take Hamish upstairs so he could settle in his bed for the night.

Hamish appeared to settle down but 2 hours later I woke up and to my surprise Hamish was walking around the bedroom and panting. I tried the obvious thing by offering water but he wasn't interested and just kept pacing around the bedroom. This woke Margaret up and being at a loss why he was constantly panting decided to do an internet search to find out what the panting signified.

We quickly found out that panting can be a sign of distress and by this time we were getting anxious and decided to call the emergency vet for advice. The vet suggested we should take Hamish straight away for a check up so we quickly dressed and set off for the vet which was about 10 miles away. The gravity of the situation hadn't sunk in and all that was going through our minds was to get some help for Hamish.

We eventually found the vets practice and after filling out a registration form took Hamish into the surgery for an examination. The vet concluded that without undergoing tests it would be difficult to conclude what the problem was so suggested that we administer pain relief and get Hamish to our local vet first thing on Monday morning.

It was now 3am on Sunday morning and at least the pain relieve medication did appear to settle Hamish down and we were hoping he would start to feel better. Unfortunately when he woke up he started panting again and we were now beside ourselves to know what was the best course of action as clearly this was something serious. We therefore made the decision to make an immediate appointment at the veterinary hospital in Wimbledon where Hamish had gone to have his eyes examined. Our appointment was treated as urgent so we set off straight after breakfast hoping that we could find out what the problem was and hopefully get some treatment. However, we were again told that without carrying out tests it would be difficult to conclude what the problem was and they felt that the best course of action was for Hamish to keep taking pain relief until we could get him to our vet on Monday morning.

At this stage we knew there was something seriously wrong with Hamish and we just wanted to get him home to make him as comfortable as possible and administer the pain relief we had been given.

The pain relief did seem to help and we all managed to get some sleep. It was however, a very long night and I was praying that Hamish would wake up and start to feel better. Unfortunately this did not happen and Hamish was now struggling to stand up and it was so distressing to see him like this as 48 hours earlier he was just fine.

Eventually we managed to contact our vet just after 8am and they told us to come to the surgery immediately so they could assess Hamish and carry out tests if necessary. The vet told us to go home and they would contact us with the results. It seemed like time had stood still waiting for the phone to ring and we continued to hope that Hamish would be ok.

The call eventually came and we received the news the devastating news that Hamish's kidneys had failed and the only course of action was to have him put to sleep. As all dog owners will know you have to put the wellbeing of your pet first and it was now the time to let him rest in peace however hard it was going to be.

We left for the vet knowing it would be the last time that we would see our beautiful Hamish the 4 legged medicine who had brought so much joy and happiness to others over the last fifteen years.

We were able to say our goodbyes to Hamish and stayed with him until his life passed away. Returning home after making the arrangements with the vet to have him cremated, so we could have his ashes back, the house seemed so empty. We just sat down and stared out of the window trying to come to terms with what had happened over the last 48 hours.

We then spent several hours phoning all our friends informing them that Hamish had been put to sleep and eventually got around to making the call we did not want to make but knew we had to phone the Hospital's volunteer manager and give her the devastating news.

Looking back it probably counts as one of the worse days of our lives and we did get some comfort from the kind messages and cards we received. The Croydon Advertiser reported the loss of Hamish with the headline *"Heartfelt tributes to volunteer Hamish"*.

We never set out for Hamish to be a Pet's as Therapy dog but looking back he was just perfect for this role. He was loving, caring, took everything in his stride and above all was our beautiful westie. Hamish will always be in our thoughts.

Above and Below Tributes to Hamish

Chapter Nineteen -
Life without Hamish

Looking back the time you have with your beloved pet seems to race by so quickly. Perhaps because Hamish had such a full life in the community the time passed by even more quickly.

When you lose your pet your routine is all over the place and the only way we could remove the pain we were experiencing was to keep busy. We were still hospital volunteers and initially we tried going around the wards we visited with Hamish but this did not work out as without Hamish it just didn't seem the same and we could not offer the comfort to patients that Hamish could provide. Having discussed this with the volunteer manager we came up with the idea of running an afternoon club whereby elderly patients do some craft, play bingo or just have a cup of tea and a chat.

This worked out very well and gave us the opportunity to tell people our story about the wonderful adventures we had with Hamish.

We also found one of the hardest things to cope with when we lost Hamish was bumping into people who would say *"where's Hamish"*. It's not an easy thing to cope with and tears would always whelm up in our eyes. By now we had received many tributes to Hamish and in a lot of ways reading the tributes was a way of looking back with pride and to some degree took the pain away.

It was a very low point in our lives and our house seemed so empty without the heart beat at our feet. The bereavement cards and tributes did to some degree help but without doubt our spirits were lifted when Croydon University hospital invited us to Crystal Palace Football Club to receive a posthumous award for Hamish in recognition of his 15 year service in the hospital as a visiting Pets As Therapy dog.

The event took place in the Football Club's entertaining space and the room was packed with other volunteers and staff members who were receiving awards as well. Hamish's award was presented to us by former Crystal Palace footballer Mark Bright who was very interested to hear what Hamish had achieved during his lifetime. Margaret was also presented with a beautiful bouquet of flowers and I accepted a certificate which stated that Hamish had achieved 105 dog years volunteering which to this day we still treasure.

By now I was approaching retirement having worked for Croydon Council for 50 years and as Margaret was already retired we thought a complete change of scenery was what we needed and without hesitation decided to move to the Isle of Wight.

We are now living in Bembridge which is a beautiful part of the Island and have a brand new detached chalet bungalow built in the New England style. We often reflect that Hamish would have enjoyed the surroundings so much and of course he has a special place in our garden where an abundance of white flowers are planted. Hamish is still with us in spirit and his photos and awards take pride of place on our walls and in our display cabinet.

Chapter Twenty – Reflections

We do hope you have enjoyed reading this story about our West Highland Terrier Hamish Mc Fee and perhaps it will inspire other dog owners to become Pets as Therapy visitors. It is a little known charity but achieves so much bringing happiness and comfort to others. If you want more information there is a wealth of it available on-line including how to get your dog registered as a Pat dog.

When we started writing this story we were not sure how it would turn out but hopefully you will agree that it does paint a picture of what one carefree westie achieved during his life. There is not a day that goes by when we do not think of Hamish but our tears have now turned to laughter re-calling all his achievements over a 15 year period.

Hamish rest in peace always in our thoughts.

Wishing on a star

Westie voted PAT
Dog of the Year

Meet Hamish
- the four legged medicine!

Hamish the Hero

WINNER

Well done
Hamish!

Hamish wins at Crufts

WINNER

Wonder Dog Hamish
saves woman in coma

He's still our winner
Crufts
Wonder vet
PAT Dog of the Year

Former champion
keeps on winning

Dr Dog's magic
medicine!

*Reminding us of some of the headlines
that made our little Hamish famous*

Above Some of Hamish's newspaper headlines
Below Meeting a young fan in the Whitgift Centre
Croydon

Hamish at the Croydon Guardian stand in the Whitgift Centre Croydon

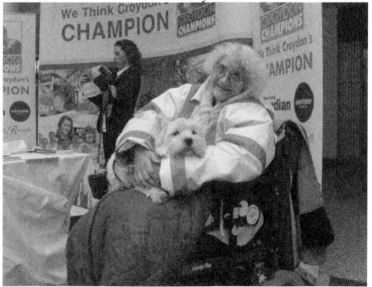

Hamish award for the Croydon Guardian Community
Champion 2010

Above Hamish meeting Pam St Clements at Crufts
Below Hamish meeting another fan

Chapter Twenty-one - Anecdotes

Looking back we all have humorous encounters with our beloved pets and Hamish was no exception and away from his working life there are other tales to tell which we hope you find amusing

<u>Awol Hamish</u>

We had a good relationship with our neighbours Pete and Ede who lived next door to us and they both loved to see Hamish and Pete always had a treat for him. We used to refer to Pete as "Uncle Pete" and Hamish always looked up when we said this. Hamish was so used to this that when we wanted Hamish to look up for a photograph we just said "Uncle Pete".

On one occasion Hamish was out in the back garden and we were inside just relaxing on a warm summers day when we both said Hamish had been outside a long time so I went to look for him and to my horror found the back gate open with no sign of Hamish.

The alarm bells started to ring so I decided to search the alleyway behind our back gate and Margaret went around the block. I thought I heard Hamish's bark coming from an adjoining street so I ventured out into the street as well. By this time we were both getting very worried so Margaret decided to go to our local park just in case Hamish was heading there and I decided to knock on Pete and Ede's door to see if they had heard anything.

When Pete opened the door to my surprise Hamish was standing in their hallway. Pete explained he was just going to bring him round to us as he was out in the garden and heard Hamish barking at this back gate. So it turned out that Hamish had not ventured into the street and just wanted a treat from Uncle Pete.

Margaret of course was still searching for Hamish and thought the best course of action was just to wait until she returned as Pete asked me in for a cup of tea. I left a note for Margaret saying where we were and eventually Margaret joined us but she was definitely not impressed with me and the next day I bought another bolt for the garden gate so Hamish would not be able to go awol again.

Hamish's encounter with a cat on holiday

Whilst I was still working full time it became a tradition that we would take Hamish on a short break holiday in the spring. One holiday in particular we stayed in the grounds of a very grand manor house in Blackdown, Dorset. It was a wonderful peaceful location and apart from the resident Housekeeper nobody else was in residence. The house keeper told us that for generations it was in the ownership of the Huntley and Palmer biscuit family but it was now owed by a city stockbroker who was restoring the manor house. Our accommodation was in a separate annex and Hamish loved exploring the grounds except for the presence of the live in cat. Hamish was not a lover of cats and back home our neighbour's cat used to tease Hamish by looking at him from the top of a shed roof.

In the grounds of Blackdown if the cat appeared Hamish would go in pursuit even though he was on an extending lead. If anyone could have seen us it must have looked like a Benny Hill sketch with Hamish running and me following up at the rear.

When we returned to our accommodation after a long day out in the countryside we were looking forward to chilling out a relaxing before having our evening meal.

To get to our front door we had to climb a set of steep wrought iron stairs so it was easier for me to carry Hamish and put him down on the first floor landing by the door. I duly opened the door and there to greet us was the Blackdown cat. Hamish was just frozen to the spot and before he could react the cat raced away. From that day on Hamish would inspect every room in the flat checking that the cat had not taken up residence.

Thief Hiding Treats

In the early years of having Hamish we still continued to have one annual holiday abroad and one of our dog walking friends Pam was happy to have Hamish for the duration of our holiday. We would never have put Hamish in a boarding kennel as he enjoyed the comforts of home too much. Hamish knew Pam was the boss and he knew he would have to behave himself. However, on one occasion Pam left Hamish with her dog Barney to get some shopping and on her return she found the pedal bin upside down and an empty tin of dog treats on the kitchen floor. Pam knew Hamish was the guilty party and assumed both Hamish and Barney had devoured the treats.

How wrong Pam was in this assumption as days later she started to come across treats hidden under chairs and cushions and quickly realised that Hamish had been hard at work carefully hiding treats for later consumption. Clever Hamish but he was still branded the "thief hiding treats

Ben Foggle meeting Hamish at Crufts

On one of our Crufts arena displays Ben Foggle was the invited guest of Pets as Therapy to present the annual award of Pat Dog of the Year. Margaret took part in the arena display and on leaving the arena she dropped her banner which narrowly missed Hamish.

Ben Foggle was standing right next to Margaret waiting to go into the arena and said *"Is your Westie ok?"*. Margaret being a fan of Ben was lost for words and was only able to say *"He's ok"*. It may have been a chance encounter but one that Margaret has never forgotten.

Hamish Surrounded!

We had a neighbour who ran a pre-school play group in our local church hall and she asked us if we would make a visit with Hamish to explain to the children what Hamish did as a Pets as Therapy dog. We bounced some ideas around and decided to keep it simple for the young children by explaining that Hamish visited people in Hospital who were not well and needed cheering up. We would also explain that Hamish had to be clean and tidy for his hospital visits and always had his Pat jacket and lead on.

The day of the talk arrived and the children were very well behaved sitting on their chairs and enjoyed hearing about Hamish's work.

Without thinking I ended the talk by foolishly saying would they like to come and stroke Hamish. In that instance there was a mini stampede of children who in an instance surrounded Hamish wanting to be the first to stroke him. Margaret quickly stepped in and explained to the children that they would have to form a line so Hamish wouldn't feel intimidated. All's well that ends well and as usual Hamish took it all in his stride and was not fazed being surrounded by 30 excited children.

It's now time to bring this story to an end and we sign off with a poem called the Rainbow Bridge. Remember to enjoy every moment you have with your beloved pet as every day is so precious. Who knows maybe it will inspire some dog owners who read this story to follow in Hamish's footsteps and bring joy and happiness to others.

THE END

The Rainbow Bridge

"When an animal dies that has been especially close to someone here, that pet goes to Rainbow Bridge. There are meadows and hills for our special friends so that they can run and play together. There is plenty of food and water and sunshine, our friends are warm and comfortable.

All the animals that have been ill or old are restored to health and vigour, those that were hurt or maimed are made whole and strong once more, just as we remember them in our dreams and times gone by.

The animals are happy and content, except for one thing, they miss someone very special to them, who has been left behind. They all run and play together, but the day comes when one suddenly stops and looks into the distance.

Their bright eyes are intent, their eager body begins to quiver. Suddenly they begin to run from the group, flying over grass, their legs carrying them faster and faster.

You have been spotted, when you and your special friend finally meet, you cling together in joyous reunion. The happy kisses rain upon your face, your hands caress again the beloved head and look once more into those trusting eyes of your pet, so long gone from life, but never in your heart.

Then you cross the Rainbow Bridge together"

Acknowledgements

To our friends Lynn and Ron who supported us throughout Hamish's life. Their photographs and DVD's capture Hamish at work and play. Also a special thanks to Lynn for all the trimming and grooming of Hamish making him look the star he was.

To our friend Val who often looked after Hamish and we used to comment that Val was running not a 5 star but 6 star hotel for dogs!

A special thanks also goes to all the Volunteer Managers at Croydon University Hospital who supported our Pets as Therapy work over the years. We take comfort that Hamish's plaque now takes pride of place in the Volunteer Managers office and he will never be forgotten.

A special mention of thanks to our previous neighbours daughters Emma and Mellissa who kindly gave up their time to help with the many Pets As Therapy road shows we held with our local co-ordinator .

We are also grateful to the support of the Hospital's stroke ward who have a plaque of Hamish on the wall opposite the nursing station. It brightened the nurse's day when Hamish was present and they referred to him as *"Dogtor Mc Fee"*.

A selection of our favourite picture

Above Hamish's plaque in the Stroke Ward at Croydon University Hospital

Below 1st Class Hamish

Hamish with friends

Hamish at a Crufts display in 2008

Above my boy Hamish

Below Barry & Margaret with Hamish

Above Hamish lights up the main arena at Crufts

Below Hamish with his Pat Dog of the year awards in 2010

Printed in Great Britain
by Amazon